THE
EMPTY-HANDED
ALTRUIST

DR. JYUTHICA. K. LAGHATE

ISBN 979-8-88805-387-4

Disclaimer

Characters, events, and incidents in this book are fictional and bear no resemblance to anyone living or dead. Any similarity found with anyone living might be coincidental.

Dedication

This book is dedicated to the lives of street children who inspite of facing devastating circumstances work hard to support their families and come out victorious. May God give them a better shelter and life.

The seeds of compassion, giving and determination sown by my beloved parents, grandparents and teachers were the sole inspiration to present this tale to the world. On a daily basis, when I see my husband, Kapil Laghate, giving so much selflessly to the needy and the expression of contentment on his face, I become energised to write for the society and bring forward through my stories, a spirit that will transform the pain in the world into moments of joy and satisfaction.

I am grateful for all such living experiences which inspire me to share my thoughts with you all.

A grand salute to the power of "Existence and Survival".

Contents

Prologue

EMPTY --

HANDED

The opulent were thrifty,

But the paupers magnanimous!

It wasn't charity of the 'Big Bucks',

But the roll of a teary eyed starving elder brother,

Feeding his baby brother, the grubs he collected from the garbs.

'Benevolence' and 'Charity',

Coming from the fist of the "EMPTY HANDED."

The world we are thriving is also an ecosystem for the surviving.

Struggling for shelter, support, nourishment and understanding.

In our luxuriant lives of cornucopia,

We lack sharing, We lack caring, We lack giving!!

This is the tale of the outer "Empty Handed" But the Innate Altruist (SELF-LESS......).

A doting boy, Manas, who takes care of his infant brother, Manan, after his parents succumb to addiction and live like mere vegetables, wolves waiting for wild drinking and lying on the roads near the gutters whilst their two boys are trying to look at the brighter picture out of a drain.

Isn't this the true emblem of positivity? To give out of your last grain of rice and be the mascot of compassion, support and kindness when you have nothing, you are empty handed, yet you fill your loved one's fists with food, security, laughter and experience.

This is a tale of kindness knowing no bounds. An elder brother carving a dream life for his baby brother, working as his shield, confidante and a limitless carer. Both these brothers shed off their rough past and become winners in their own regard.

A story that creates hope out of ashes and endeavours to imbibe the grit, resolve, patience and goodness in souls that are troubled but not emotionally broken.

For me, Manas is the 'Empty Handed Altruist', a boy who became a man at a tender age, shouldering all the responsibilities that his father should have and became a cornerstone for his family, friends and fraternity.

Let us celebrate his spirit; let us celebrate his empty handed lion heartedness that he indulged in at an early age where he sacrificed his dreams for his brother and mother.

Let us acknowledge the power of kindness, a silent force that can fill lives of children with hope, strength and direction.

Kind Regards,

Dr. Jyuthica. K. Laghate

Manan's Birth or My Rebirth???????

Amma (Mom) was lying on the side of the Deccan signal with a few lady officers crying their hearts out to drive us, our family of four, away from this wee footpath that was our abode for the last 4 years.

I faintly remember Baba(Dad), as almost half dead, stinking like a rotten animal with a breath teeming with alcohol that any halimeter would have detected several feet away and Amma weeping like a small child who was hungry for days . The cries were because of her excruciating labour pains.

What a heart wrenching experience for a mother who is so helpless, broke, vulnerable and about to deliver her child amidst this deafening traffic, angry and iniquitous eyes looking at her with despise and abhorrence. Some ladies were passing the footpath and someone, sane, just threw her shawl and howled, "Take this and save us from the shame."

That shawl, though flung patronisingly, was her saving grace…In the midst of her tears, a faint smile line emerged and my heart pounding slowed down a bit. May be Manan wanted to come in this world, feeling a little protected under the warmth of that shawl… that motherly wool.

After the immense trauma, physical, mental, social concocted together, Amma finally delivered a chubby, not so dusky boy on this metropolitan street of Pune. In the modern scheme of things, sophisticated mothers have the liberty to give themselves some pampering, some serious empathy and concern for their postpartum depression which is quite natural for a girl suddenly becoming a mother in the miniscule of a second. But my Amma, as blessed as she was, did not even have a supportive bed or linen or a doting husband to be by her side during her delivery. Even as a young boy, I could horrifically picture her life close to stray dogs where the females deliver in the open, left alone to be testimonies of their debilitating pain, suffocation and insecurity.

I ran to the end of the street to get Frooti (mango drink) for my extremely enervated mother with her new born crying next to her and she did not have a bone left in her to feed him. That moment, something churned in my belly, a kind of salient force just erupted, the hibernated elder brother and fatherly instinct that it was, I quickly sprinted to the milk man and begged him for a small milk pouch and took it on loan ('Udhari' as they call in Hindi).

It was my little angel's birth and my rebirth as a 6 year old elder brother, a ragamuffin, who had the biggest chamber of emotion in his heart and whose life was filled with utter joy and exuberance that his baby brother had arrived with soft feet to complete his family looking for atleast a faint light at the end of this hideous tunnel. Manan's infantile innocence used to fill some smiles in my life which otherwise was struggle and endless toil by sunrise right until midnight. I used to sell small plastic toys and roses at the main Deccan signal.

These cars and bikes used to come at startling speeds and somehow used to brake at the signal. I, with my expectant, watery eyes, yellow sclera, muddy shirt on a bath less body, extremely dry, gingery ruffled hair used to knock all cars with an incandescent hope that someone will buy my beautiful pink and yellow roses, my rare plastic toys and provide us with atleast a tenner to buy our family favourite 'Wada Pav' (Favourite Indian Snack). It was rainy season; the entire street was filled with puddles due to torrential rains and our street home was dilapidated.

A home with no roof, just some rugs, some stale water bottles, a pair of torn and tattered clothes and a permanent—Baba always high on alcohol. God knows! Where on earth he stole the money to get a bottle or two every four days but the audacity of his wretched soul that he never offered food to his wife or kids or never even held me or the new baby in his arms.

I used to pity mom at that tender age too. Why did she marry such a vile man? Who chose him for her? Did she deserve this absolute devastation?

So many of us, the street children, are products of such desolate mothers left bare to face the harsh realities of poverty, exploitation and massacre.

The rain, today evening, was on an anger spree , hitting us laterally, every time sending chills off our spine. Manan, a month old baby, was weeping on end and mom had given up. To make things worse, the wet clothes made her catch fever and cold and she couldn't hold Manan due to her scorching skin. She handed Manan to me and uttered, "Manas, now you have to look after Manan till I feel better and she literally went in to a stupor, she had not eaten since a day, was shivering due to the wet cold and was just disconsolate to say the least.

Baba, nothing new, merely woke up, rubbing his eyes, after almost a day, howling with hunger.

For his young thirties, he was merely able to stand on his two feet and demanded from me , a poor 6 year old, to hunt for food- beg, borrow, steal, kill- but satiate his hunger. I buckled up courage and refused. He was boiling with anger and tried to throw the water bottle at me, thinking it was glass.

Good Lord! I was saved by his mere lack of identification and judgement. This is what, excessive quantities of poisonous alcohol with no food and only reproach in the heart does to you.

You lose it!!! He did too!!

I will never forget that pouring … From outside, with water flooding our rugs and my intrinsic sobbing and salty tears that no gentleman could see or come close to me and give me a reassuring hug. But, I was literally clinching Manan. As an elder boy, I was nothing but steadfast to protect him from all ills, family and otherwise. I quickly tugged him under my shirt, how tiny he was and ran to the Frooti vendor, got it and threw it on my Dad, unwillingly. If I hadn't, the water on our rugs might have become blood red. So violent and reckless my father was!

Mom was still lying torpid on the wet rug, not responding to Manan's shouting or mine. The entire birthing process with no food and inclement weather had taken a toll on her jaded soul. She needed time. She needed caring. She needed understanding. To expect that from Baba would have been the height of positivity. But, I was there, in my frail stature, standing against the wall, covering Manan, looking fondly at my mother to wake up and atleast be there with us in the moment of grief or whatever.

I again felt like reborn: an elder brother struggling to protect his younger brother and mother along with futile attempts of evading from his father. If birth is challenging, as they say, rebirth is wreathing the self to take a new form, a new role, a new stance.

Manan's Walk Into Literacy...

From struggling to even have a separate rug to sleep or a soft pillow to support his brainy head, Manan was my partner in: 'Life Lessons of Being at the Rock Bottom and Not Having a Life Jacket to Float.' However, as a child, he had that immense optimism, laughter, mischief and inquisitiveness in him. Every day, when I used to run till my bare feet cracked, he used to be busy picking some petals of left over flowers and made some designs out of them. He giggled by himself, forgetting and ignoring whatever drastic and uncivil was happening around him.

I don't recount him ever going near our father or crying because of his belligerent behaviour nor did he pity mom. He was an eternal optimist, whose smile lit me up at the darkest hour. He was a blessing, a beatific one for me! Although, I had the wits, my parents did not possess the will and the money to admit me in a school.

I mean, in this age of free education for underprivileged kids, my parents, still didn't feel, education and hygiene worthy over ignorance, evil and filth.

At those down trodden moments, I used to question the existence of God, his omnipotent compassionate spirit but Manan was always this virtuous angel who was God sent to pick me up from trash and take me to the world of hope and dreams, however fantastical they felt whilst in muck. I was motivated than ever to change the ignorance streak of the family and wanted to send Manan to school.

I still fondly remember, two days continuously, I was imagining him vividly, wearing a clean uniform, polished shoes, nicely combed hair and walking holding my hand to the nearby Municipality school. I used to jump with joy, every time this little one's schooling image popped in front of my dreamy and weary eyes. This dream needed to be a solid reality!!

I, somehow, dressed myself, decent enough, to visit a nearby school with my boy.

Atta boy! I can't tell you, how it felt in words: an eclectic mixture of elation, nerves, expectation, love, fear, possessiveness and insecurity. I was shaken to the core. What if my boy is harassed or mocked for his background? What if he is not able to cope up with the studies? Will he learn to abuse and do crazily vain things?

I felt more anxious than Amma and Baba. We had Manan's interview in the neighbouring school with the Principal, Mrs. Athavale.

We reached her office at 10 am sharp. She was quite shocked to see two kids holding each other's hand entering her room completely tremulous. She had a plain smile on her face, her bifocal spectacles hanging on her nose, her hair, all gray being a silent witness to her knowledge train and her attire, simple and understated. An ideal teacher's persona! She asked us to sit on the wide wooden chairs, without cushions, in front of her. There was an educational poster in Marathi on her desk. She asked Manan his name and address.

I anxiously swallowed my saliva, almost feeling thirsty like never before. Manan answered correctly. But for address, he said, "Don't know Bai (Marathi word for madam)."

We sit on the Deccan signal for days. That is our address I guess. There was this threatening pause......
Two of us looking at her and she staring at us, with her eyeballs, filled with little water, about to trickle, but she conducted herself with composure and stolidity and uttered, "Beta (Son), You come to school from Monday." She asked him Marathi names of couple of fruits and animals. Manan, incidentally knew them, but his pronunciations were raw, his accent, very crass.

I thanked Almighty by looking in the sky, had seen it, when some people kissed their lockets or looked at the sky when they were overjoyed or achieved something.

Finally, the first boy in our long, abjected family of generations and generations on the street was going to attend formal school right from nursery stage.

How relieved I was would be an understatement and injustice to the power of that moment. Nothing can faintly describe what I felt at that exact, finite moment, when I looked at my adorable Manan. I thanked Madam somehow and ran out of her office.

The moment we saw the playground ahead of the porch, we rushed there, yelled and weeped with joy. Our voices were as strong as any motivational rhetoric by a Guru, the spirit in us felt resurrected and we were confident from the core that Manan's walk into literacy is not going to be just about words and knowledge but about erasing the indelible sorrows with ink of golden happiness and future success.

People wait to return to their sweet homes and ours was a footpath corner. Neatly decorated by us brothers, resonating a positive vibe like no other converting all harsh experiences into life manuals of crushing them and moving on our path. My role now was ever more significant, since Manan was going to need daily support for managing his school, his food and more so his will to fight this terrible neighbourhood of alcoholics and offenders and concentrate on progress instead.

Manan's first day at school is still etched permanently in one corner of my heart that is reserved permanently just for his life, growth and cheer.

Every day, he went to school with lot of enthusiasm and gave me this tightest hug. I was the person he only cared for.

Our parents, Amma and Baba, were fading from his life like past meetings with strangers. I didn't blame him for his dispassionate disposition towards them. In his times of need, they demanded more attention because of their crumbling lives and conversion into a more bestial than human existence.

To say the least, we did not have ideal role models in our parents. But, that kind of rekindled the burning desire in me, more and more, to be my Manan's true hero. May sound egotistical, but I enjoyed the sheer intensity of the boosting pride that his affection and twinkling eyes provided me. It was the best fuel for my day and I did not leave any stone unturned to create noble examples for him to follow. That was my nostrum for his debilitating experiences from his blood relatives. Manan's school was another silver lining for our dark cloud and I can say, his school days were the best days of our street life.

From Four We Became Three...

Amma was feeling a bit better with the school activities of Manan and everyday gave a pat on my back, teary eyed as always. In her small existence, her two sons were her real bolsters. Now, she could resort to Manan for explaining her simple Maths and counting. Manan had passed Junior and Senior Kg. It was his 5th birthday on the 15th of January. We never knew what a birthday celebration was. It still sends chills off my spine when I recollect the birth of my tiny brother, struggling to bear the freezing cold of the street floor and not getting mother's milk or nourishing food throughout his infancy. His cries still echo in my ears and everytime make me overwrought, howsoever, strong, I pretend to be in front of Amma and Manan.

Manan's birthday morning was just another day for us. Manan's class teacher, Miss Malini Joshi, made it special by wishing him right in the first period and handed a bag of chocolates to him to take some home and distribute the rest to his classmates. I was eagerly waiting outside the school to pick him up. What an unpropitious time that was to break the news to him that Baba had not woken up since morning. As soon as the school bell rang, Manan came out of the school with his signature bunny smile and quickly came around to hug me from behind.

His exact words, "Manas Dada (big brother), my class teacher gave me chocolates, she didn't give you. See, I am her favourite with his mischievous twinkling eyes and charming gaze. My heart literally thudded to convey the so called tragic news of our father passing away in sleep due to alcohol overdose.

But Manan, as expected, changed the topic. I was trying to explain him that the police have arrived on our street, we need to go and support our mother. Almost, oblivious, his strides were as gentle and slow as everyday. However, the moment we reached the edge of the street and when he saw the sheer numbers of the crowd, the police standing in clusters and mom's shrieking, he started trembling and clinched my right hand like never before.

The moment had dawned on to him that Baba won't be there physically now and forever. As it is, Baba's vituperative behaviour since Manan's birth had already prepared him mentally long ago to imagine our family of only three. Still, encountering death, even of your adversary, is not easy to say the least. I can acutely collect the face of my mother that moment. Pallor, sinking eyes, a huge band of dark circles, plenty of wrinkles, lips dry and sticking on to each other, she personified a lady, worn out completely with the continuous assailing of life in all its forms.

Appallingly though, despite the array of exploitative mechanisms thrown at her by her husband, she still weeped and weeped with care.

What an absolutely giving soul she was? Hard to trust that the modern vicious life still bears witness to such darling individuals who are nothing but epitomes of sacrifice, goodness and support. My whole body and just not my heart swelled with pride and reverence for my dearest mother , a smelly street dweller for the masses, but an extremely balmy, kind mother for us who with her rough, unmoistured earthen hands caressed us and made us feel like the "Chosen Ones".

The utter irony of human life, sometimes, people very near to you might not be dear because of their repetitive abusive behaviour. Me and Manan, both felt a bit of relief or a cathartic peaceful feeling when our father was cremated.

That void and silence felt good instead of morose and mom, too, was kind of getting recuperated from all the physical, mental, economical and social abuse that was packaged in the strangest phenomenon of her life: Marriage. That made me rather have a strong negativity about marriages.

I questioned, "Why people get married and then spoil each other's life with battles and aggression? Then why do they call it love and are connected for life?

How can love be so violent and destructive?" At that tender age of 13, I had decided, not to get married till I find someone who is an absolute angel or unreally good. Not that I knew, how testing and complex, human love really is …

Three months after Baba's demise, our life was a tad better in all regards. Mom's health and mood was sanguine, she was helping me on a daily basis in selling more flowers and toys. We had systematically divided the areas between us and were toiling hard to earn and save as much as we could for our subsistence and our Manan's future.

For the first time in thirteen years, on 20th Feb 2006, as a family we had three full meals and I undoubtedly felt on 'Cloud nine'. For many, having three meals is a given, for us, a priviledge! Manan's and my health also was improving; we had developed some colour on our faces, a little fat on our cheeks and bums. All in all, a happy- chappy start for our renewed existence.

From four, we became a joyous squad of more healthy, eating and living three. Life when four was no life really; it was a mere encumbrance…

A full family is supposed to be one joyous, complete family. For us, it was an abyss with no sign of light and life.

For me and Manan, being three was a blessing in disguise almost like death giving birth to a renewed existence. It is here, where an inchoate mind was being molded to understand the harsh ironies of living and perhaps this bitterness went on to bake the sweetness of creative fervour in me as a young adult.

For a Change: The Elder One Idolised the Younger One

Manan was now 7 years old and I was a kicking 13. We had reached a point in our street career where in, we could afford three meagre meals and buy a thing or two for us. Life wasn't too bad anymore. I sensed an immediate opportunity in this scenario and wanted desperately to begin schooling like my charming, young Manan. One day, I somehow gathered all the courage and wits, in whatever bits that I possessed and went to meet Manan's principal, our beloved, Athavale madam.

She was beaming to see me after a long time and welcomed me with a smile like never before. The first few minutes, she spoke volumes about Manan's progress in school, his inclination towards art and craft and his consistent improvement in mathematics and social studies. I was smiling so much that my cheeks were hurting and a bit stiff, couldn't help but respond to madam's kindness and compassion for my little brother.

I, with an extremely anxious timbre in my already faint voice uttered, "Madam, now that we are earning a little better than before, I, too, want to join school and learn from the best like you."

"

I can never forget the expression on Athavale madam's face. She had almost become flushed with joy mixed with watery eyes and the specks hanging on her straight nose, she kind of placed her spectacles at their proper position, gathered herself and replied, "Beta! You are always welcome in our school since you are the only boy who has shown the real steel of a man. You personify the ideal youth of this city and I can't wait for you to join from first standard itself. No need of pre-primary education for a boy like you who has mastered the degree of life and its challenges already."

Her extended dialogue was the best motivational talk I have or will ever receive. That confidence and esteem that she instilled in me, her sheer faith on my sacrifices and affection for my family was enough for a dreamer like me to fill my heart and body with vigour, resolve and inspiration and embark on my new journey on foot:

Manas's entry into Manan's school. A reverse paradigm, where the elder one idolises the younger bud.

I rushed home; Manan was eating his rice and dal in a small disposable bowl. I picked him up, exuberantly and told him the biggest news of my life. I was going to study in his school from Monday. His reaction was epic; he jumped and giggled and hugged our mother and shouted, "Dada is going to be with me the whole day in school.

We will meet during lunch break and eat and study together. I don't need anymore to hunt for friends. I am tired to convince classmates to eat with me or take me in their group. If dada is in school, I don't need anyone."

Those appeasing words still created that stream of sorrow and I went in to a bout of crying , remembering my age old struggles vis-à-vis Manan's triumphs of reaching school and fighting the string of daily battles there of facing rejection or disparage from the more priviledged lot. My hands were filled with goose bumps, my heart was racing, my throat was parched. How much will I get ridiculed or mocked in school?

I was going to be in first grade at the age of 13. The tallest boy in the class with weakest curriculum knowledge, training and a pauper qualification.

This challenge was heaped on the top of so many that had been hurled vilifyingly at me by the jaws of destiny. As if the street problems had waned, that this new one was earnest to surface. Destiny's children like me are tested not every month or year but every moment. In theory, all motivational highs out of defeating one battle and woe after the other seems like a flashy exemplification but in a hard and more hard hitting reality, every issue feeds on a piece of your heart and is waiting for your carcass: bare, wounded and decimated.

Somewhere, in the truest of feelings, I was an emotional skeleton.

My tender bones were obliterated by hits and impacts of sorrow, expectation, struggle and pain. At 13, my soul sometimes felt wrinkled, my body felt emaciated and mind haggard. Yet, the spirit of being human is what is truly relentless and separates us from the rest. No can macerate us mentally unless we choose to do so.

With a renewed vigour, school bells were going to ring in my life bringing tunes of hope and a prospective future. I must thank Manan for properly keeping all his textbooks from first standard. The Sunday before starting school was superbusy since I had to distribute the selling duties to mom and some other street buddies. I was very much concerned about whether they would give 100% in their work and fulfil the daily revenue targets.

But, in life one has to delegate duties and trust otherwise life could be a nightmare carrying the burden of all the tasks.

I had become preachy right before school, to be good and not drink at any cost, to dress up in clean outfits and not wallow in mud, to be serious, attentive and more than anything, to have patience and endurance to face the multitude of reactions, bad, better or worst from the classmates or teachers. I had done my moral homework and how!

My class teacher, Miss Megha Gokhale, was welcoming from day one. She would always repeat whatever, I did not understand and at the end of the day would call me in her staff room and gave a gentle pat on my back, saying, "Beta, don't worry, it is better late than ever. Just because you are doing grade-I at this age, doesn't mean you have no scope or potential.

It just means, you have reached the destination a little late than others, but the sprint in your stride and the agility of your thoughts and determination will take you places. That is my promise to you, my dear." I bowed down to take her blessings and felt for the first time that elders are real cornerstones of a child's future. Till then, my set of elders, my parents were mere consanguinities with a related blood but the farthest unfamiliar minds and souls. I don't remember, by any stretch of my constricted memory, about touching my parent's feet. Unfortunately, they had never proved to be good role models. Everytime, a ray of joy touched my life, there was a streak of gloom adhered to it, just so closely. Isn't this another paradox of human existence? Every joy has a reflection of sorrow and otherwise.

Yet, I had learnt in an extremely hard way, the path to control my nerves, emotional outbursts or dolour.

School was by far the best experience of my formative years, howsoever, late it began. It felt like 5 in first standard and never out of place.

The School Finishing Line for Manan and for Me?

Manan had grown into this handsome, medium heighted boy with twinkling black eyes, snow white teeth, dark brown, unoiled hair and a dimple on his left cheek that just added so much of charm to his already dazzling charisma. No one would recognise that he came from such unkempt corners of street dwelling.

By this time, we had been promoted from a roofless street existence to a metallic roof hut near the Parvati hills, about 3-4 kms from Deccan signal, our prima abode. It was Manan's SSC year and good lord! He got a tiny corner space with a zero watt bulb to study. I mean a roofed house was no less than a palace for us. We had a right cornered kitchen with a stove and some humble utensils: disposable plates and bowls. From drinking heavily sweet Frooti and spoiling our guts with worms and infections, we had transcended to a more healthy and nutritious diet with roti, dal and rice, some leafy vegetable or an egg as a delicacy once a week.

Our bodies were so quick to positively respond to this food and both of us had become a little plump than our previously over ripped bodies with popping ribs and bent femurs.

I was in grade 4 now and everyday became more and more keen to perform well in studies and art based activities in school. Our school has opened up a small business unit for underprivileged school students. We were given rigorous training about candle making, creating environment friendly incense and Diwali lamps out of recycled material.

Everyday, few of us were chosen to spend an hour after school to help the school unit manufacture these items.

I had found a new passion and enjoyed making fragrant candles in rainbow colours. On the last Saturday of the month, the school used to arrange a fair in which the items were sold at very reasonable prices and the student with maximum sales was given a prize bonus. I had won two consecutive bonuses for the January and February months. I had learnt to save this money (Rs. 1200) that I earned, in an earthen pot shaped piggy bank.

We called that "Matka" and had decided that we would open it on my birthday on 20th March and go out with mother and treat her with some Paani Puri and Bhel(Famous Indian snacks).

Chaat was our favourite food and everytime, Manan and me crossed the Paanipuri stall bhaiya (person) our mouth used to water waiting for the sweet-sour out of this world Paani Puris. But, atleast, now we were not completely penniless and could savour them later.

Time flew as usual. Before we knew, Manan's final exam was round the corner. He was literally burning midnight oil and preparing for his SSC boards. I was a proud elder brother, who was kind of getting in the groove of primary education with my 4th grade examination approaching.

My exams got over by 24th March and daily, I was accompanying Manan to his exam centre, a small Government school near our house. I made sure, he had his breakfast, a little heavy than always plus made him drink lime water every single day. It was typically dry and hot summer of Pune and he used to get more dehydrated with the stress.

His papers such as English, Marathi, Hindi and Social Sciences were over and his dreaded Mathematics and Science were still left and scheduled after a break of 5 days. I was naturally better at calculations than Manan, I still am. I used to sit with him and give him moral support that he so badly needed.

Amma used to make piping hot dal, vegetable curry and bhakri for him, a local type of roti with jowar. She said, "Manan, one bhakri a day will keep tiredness away." We laughed and laughed and called our Amma, "The Eternal Filmy One." Today was 25th April, the finish line for the SSC race. Manan and I had planned to walk to the nearby park and enjoy some street food after his exam.

At sharp 2 pm, his Mathematics paper got over. He somehow, packed his bags shabbily and just ran out of his examination hall, as fast as he possibly could. I was standing in front of him near the cycle stand. He was overjoyed. The paper went well than expected. He exclaimed, "Dada, I will definitely score a first class this time." My feeling was that of a proud parent, waiting earnestly for that day, when his or her offspring becomes an achiever or starts their promising journey of development.

We couldn't help our big blobby tears rolling on our tanned cheeks; there was laughter amidst a far cry. We had seen the rough of the rough, the gross grotesque harshness of the streets, the exploitation, the malnourishment, you name the ill and we had encountered it.

But, his SSC landmark, whitewashed all that grief into an everlasting moment of elation and pride. We bought some cold drink and toffees on our way to our residence and wanted to give Amma a surprise. As soon as we reached our house, we asked her to close her eyes and gave a disposable, big glass filled with Pepsi and a medium sized Dairy milk to her. Manan smiled, "Mom, my paper went very well and I am going to make you proud with my high scores."

Mom opened her eyes, hugged Manan and me so tightly that we were almost short of breath. Her happiness knew no bounds;she promised that she will cook our favourite egg curry for dinner.

Right from birth till his tenth grade, Manan, gave me so much to cherish and relish that perhaps my son or daughter won't be able to give me .

As anticipated, on 2nd June, in the morning, we hurriedly went to the school to collect Manan's marksheet. As any other extremely anxious student, Manan's cold hands were snuggled into my sweaty ones. We provided the office administration staff his hall ticket and that waiting for five minutes felt like five hours. He rapidly shuffled the marksheets that were not arranged alphabetically. I was trying to ask him repeatedly, "Kaka, did you get Manan's sheet."The man, after sorting the lot, sighed, "Got it little ones. Congratulations! Manan has passed and that too with a first class. We need a box of sweets. Your brother has provided an ideal example for all the street boys; they can come here, study their heart out and expect a greater result. We are dream makers son!"

We went home…I think, we were floating in air, not strolling. Mom was at the door, taking rounds and looking at the road, eagerly, for us. As soon as she saw us from a distance, she came out running, faster than us, folding her saree, with her heavy chappals, and caressed us both.

Manan touched her feet and hugged her tightly, lifted her up and we had our trio celebration of his scintillating success. The neighbours, too, were on cloud nine. Their street boy had successfully surpassed a crucial academic landmark. They had thousand dreams about Manan tantamount to ours. Manan was keen to pick up commerce and then later do an MBA. The dude had skyrocketing dreams and why not?

Manan's result was ever more inspiring for me. I was determined to score atleast 75% in my tenth grade, and how intensely was I waiting to enter 10th. Finally after 4 years, my finish line of secondary school had befolded. Manan was already in third year of his college. The roles had now reversed. He was the old soul, teaching me social sciences, taking my revision, giving me daily timed tests. His experience and tips were saviour for me in the examination.

My exams, too, finished in the last week of April. This time, we had a celebration week and not a day. We ate few luscious mangoes and melons. We played cricket on the street. We went to the local chaat stall to binge on some paani puris and bhel. Occasionally, we used to make this highly saccharine lime water and drink it like a lemonade.

Finally, the result bell rang. It was 5th of June. Manan, now, was taller than me, more serious looking, dreamy, fellow.

He was dressed, very prim and proper, like a wannabe, was holding my hand and pacified me, "Dada, don't panic and worry. You have worked too hard to fail or not get your desired score. You are and always have been 'the winner' for me."

His words were like elixir in this fatally stressful moment. All kinds of thoughts, raced in my mind, like a three hour thriller. What if I fail? I just pass or not score well in the subjects I have given my heart and soul for.

The admin uncle was still the same, bespectacled, middle framed, fair gentleman with the thick moustache, Mr.Kamble. I asked him, "Kaka, have the marksheets arrived." He remembered both of us and was pleasantly surprised to see Manan, so tall, handsome and confident. He turned his face to me and added, "Beta, don't worry. Your incredible support and good karma for your family will work wonders in the result. You will pass well."

I got hold of my marksheet at 1 pm after standing in the line for almost two hours. The colourful appearance of the document, the boldly printed remarks section, First class with distinction, took me in a fantasy land. I had scored 77.5% percent, two percent more than I had expected.

All this while, being a senior one in a batch of little ones had instilled that sense of diffidence and underestimation of my potential. I thought delayed study equals to substandard performance. But, I was wrong, categorically and to my pleasantest surprise.

Manan felt like a big boy and kept on staring at my marksheet with his nose swollen in pride.

He was speechless for almost fifteen minutes and was just glaring at me with his piercing, lovely eyes. It was a flashback reel. All my struggles, sacrifices, placing him ahead of all my dreams had dawned on to him. He gave me a Hershey Hug, the warmest one and whispered in my ears, "For the world, you have scored a distinction but for me you have gained a gold medal in rising above ashes and proving yourself like a lifetime champion. Dada, your kindness, talent and actions make me feel so humbled, so small in front of your pure, real pristine heart of gold."

I enjoyed all that escalated praise; my class teacher, Gokhale madam, came personally to the office to congratulate me. She held my face fondly and averred, "Son, whatever money you need for your further education, I will arrange it. Our school has lot of tie ups with sponsors and I will make sure, I get you a fully paid scholarship for your next 5 years of education. But, please don't stop studying, Manas.

You are a gifted painter and a degree in visual art or graphic art would be ideal."

We went home. I was contemplating; Manan's finish line and mine went well, without bumps. First challenge was overcomed and college years waited with a bated breath for me.

I was soaring to take a leap as high as I wished in dreams with open eyes, whilst making people's birthdays and anniversaries memorable with colourful roses and my sweaty hands holding the stems of rose bunches, fragrant and attractive, but with so many thorns that manier times would accidentally prick me and often be witness to my pale reddish blood with less 'haem' but amply thick due to anguish and strife.

Born Thrice

My date of birth was 20th March, my rebirth was 5th January (Manan's birthday) and I think, I am the truly blessed one to be born thrice in college.

This time, it is a story of a larva becoming a beautiful butterfly with shades of love, determination, growth and peace. As a matter of fact, college days were transformative, everything in the Arts stream in my iconic, Fergusson college was magical. Right from the old British architectural charm, wide corridors, black stone Victorian buildings, huge amphitheatre, everything was just right for an art lover like me.

I can imagine how Picasso felt inspired out of the mundane. Inspiration was there like oxygen, subtle, invisible but there all the time.

Every morning, I used to walk for 3 km and take a bus from Tilak Road, right in the city centre. It used to take around 25 minutes to get near my college bus stop.

Although, Manan, too, was in the same college, thanks to our school teacher's persistent efforts to get us full paid scholarships, he was in his final year of Bachelor of Commerce programme and used to meet me quite rarely due to his busy schedule.

God had started to be kind to us and he had already landed up in a part time job as an accounts assistant in a supermarket. His salary paved way to a one room kitchen house, around 1 km from our previous home. We were climbing ladders, just like the 'Snakes and Ladders' game, sometimes a five would provide us with a long ladder like this and on other occasions we would come back to square one. But, recent past was more stable, infact our time from school days itself changed and for better.

A fully fed stomach leads to a stable, thinking fellow and both of us were able to sustain our studies and part time work with poise and satisfaction. Being an artist, I had joined an art gallery in the heart of the city as a gallery administration assistant.

I used to spend hours together looking at the stunning paintings of other artists, sometimes used to rebuff a few for lack of panache and at other times used to get engrossed in managing the inventory and expenses. All in all, evening four hours used to pass in a flash.

Morning college was a blessing! I distinctly remember our first English lecture that used to be my favourite.

Like many Indian kids, I was fascinated by the language, the colour of the people who spoke it and the ever distant dreamland or what we called, "foreign".

I had learnt basic English in school and now was the time to brush it more by making more sophisticated friends: needless to say, wanted some posh friends as girls too.

But, who would look at this humble, oiled hair, poor boy, who just had two pairs of jeans and few shirts, an odd tee-shirt and simple slippers on his wide feet.

We had meagre resources; but the world around us was luxuriant.

Students from well to do families attended Fergusson; those days and perhaps, still, Fergusson college is a style statement. Retrospectively, that helped though.

We got a chance to hang out with folks that knew how to carry themselves, where to eat, how to impress girls and so on. Apart from the academic lessons, lot was in store the whole day. Manan and I sometimes used to encounter each other briefly near Pune's most famous restaurant, Vaishali, coz that is right in front of our college.

One of my richer friends, Vikas, had a richer heart too. He used to treat me every other day for a coffee or an idli sambar(South Indian dish) or sometimes toast butter. I used to feel so loved, never felt the void of a girlfriend amidst company of very endearing and honest friends who made sure that they brought smiles on my face on trying days.

Well, I don't say college was transcendental without a reason. Friendship was one, studies was second and part time work the vital third.

Amidst this hustle bustle, I was getting an hour or two to paint. With limited budget, fire in the belly and inspiration from the variegated shades of experience, I started experimenting with water colours, the most economical painting medium yet the most vivid. Like so many others, natural scenery was my first muse and I spent first few months to practice simpler, easily replicable drawings. The best part about the process was the calmness and joy that I felt every single time while drawing and colouring. Choosing colours, highlighting the boundaries were my favourites.

My drawing book started accompanying me to college. During free periods, which we invariably got every single day, I was resolute to utilise this time and polish my painting skills.

As told earlier, Fergusson was filled with picturesque spots and I now kind of switched towards sketching buildings with black and white shading. Black and white art was bare and real. It reminded me every now and then about the candid, brutal experiences I had as a child but sketching was like a shadow of my heart and soul. All the black experiences were converted into the snow white patches in the drawings. I had started enjoying this pencil art much more than the multi-coloured water colour exhibits.

Every artist, big or small, well known or anonymous has a groove, an element that is so him: no one can copy or recreate that. Remember, Mr.Hussain's horses, Raja Ravi Verma's princesses or Picasso's experimentation with geometry.

All of them are peerless, unique and surface an aspect of the artist's personality. I was seeking mine. Who am I as a painter? What do my paintings convey? What does my medium emanate? Deep inside, I had to answer these questions: uninhibitedly and lucidly. I think, this is what age does to you. It broadens and sharpens your perspective.

Final year at Fergusson was by far the best year of my life. I represented college for three state and one national art fest. I can say, the learnings and exposure that I got in these competitions created a solid plinth for my artistic endeavours later. For the national fest, I picked up my own story as the theme. A pencil sketch highlighting a street abode with a bunch of kids picking roses and running on the street. The painting was intense with lot of human figurines and had to be planned in a way that the message is clear, churning and impactful. I spent almost a week doing it part by part. The festival was at Jaipur and from Fergusson, only ten of us were participating.

I had to rely on my savings for the train ticket but luckily my rail fare got covered by my piggy pot. Issue was of the living cost there. College had arranged a decent hotel for us for a period of three days. To say, that I was excited and anxious would be an understatement. This was my first trip outside Pune, that too, by train. I came home and broke the news to my family. Manan and mom were over the moon. Mom said, "This festival is a golden opportunity for you. Make the most of it son." The day of travelling finally arrived. From early morning itself, I was fidgety, checking whether my painting is packed properly and I was constantly walking inside my tiny living room bumping on some furniture corners thinking about how the festival would go. Will I be able to answer visitor's questions? Will my painting be amongst the worst? Am I good enough and streak of such negative questions…

I think, this is the ubiquitous saga of human nature wherein at every opportunity most of us feel so stressed and insecure that we forget what our true power and talents are. I mean, nerves get the better of us so many times. But, this time, I was determined not to let the chance go astray. I had to make a mark. After all, my entire story was real in blood, sweat and tears. It would appeal to the masses in the visual art format.

We started off for our journey to Jaipur. All ten of us were from different streams and years. Yet, a common bond of extreme love for art and expression tied us together.

The train journey was picturesque and full of new experiences. Drinking hot tea getting down at junctions, having pattice in the train, eagerly awaiting packed dinner from the train pantry and above all, chatting for hours together with all the participants made the journey more inspiring, endearing and reminiscing.

My inner self always was trying to understand the other participants and if anybody needed any help during the journey, I used to be more than glad to assist them.

I think, caring for others comes very naturally to me and the tendency to strive for other's benefit was inherent from Manan's birth. Some of my friends in the train had still not completed their colouring and were utilising the breaks at the stations to fill in some bits.

It was some fun, aligning the paintings, managing the wobbly train and maintaining the fine balance between not letting the colours spill yet fill the nooks and corners.

That is the 'art of living', isn't it? One has to manage several tasks, so many challenging ones, take ill treatment in one's stride and keep moving. You can't stop and wait for everything to be rosy.

We were almost close to Jaipur and last few minutes of the journey were emotional. We all did not want the journey to end. But we had to climb down the train and commence our new destination, "Art Fest – A celebration of our dreams."

Had I imagined my life to be so ideal and full of positivity sitting on those street corners, starving for hours and getting bridled by slews of abuse and maltreatment?

Life changes and so do you. This lesson of existence was eye opening. I suddenly began to gauge the power of my new, abundant life with art, education, friends and a much happier family than before.

Something inside my gut just told me, "Wait and watch, Manas. Life is going to change for better in 360 degrees." I strongly believe in gut instinct because that worked for me from an age when I did not even understand, what an instinct is or planned thought. That is how, I always tried to find a link between my joyful experiences and the existence of God. Jaipur art festival was one of the gifts, lord bestowed on me, I guess.

The festival went better than I expected. There were lots of visitors who loved my art form and theme and specially took my contact details to enquire about whether I was going to do more of such work.

That itself was like the biggest boost for my humble art.

But, as they say, 'Truth is eternal and it prevails'.

The candor of my suffering and miserable existence was true to the core and that shone like hundred dazzling suns. I had heard before that truth always sells and I had got a full proof for that. The festival ended on a high note and we were back to Pune with renewed vigour and distended hearts.

I Dared to be an "Altruist"

After my successful graduation and Manan's timely completion of MBA, we decided to start a co-venture, a small NGO that would look after street children. Manan was a trained management professional and had developed solid negotiation skills to get key people and financial resources on board. Our journeys had been beautifully shaped in our school by our beloved principal and teachers and we grabbed the power of that time to visit them and discuss about our ambitious plans.

Athavale Madam, our principal, was more than glad to see us. At every landmark that she saw us, she would stare at us for minutes, with watery big eyes, wipe her glasses and would fondly entertain all our discussions and demands. Both of us were destiny's children handed over to these angels from school. Madam did talk about the possibility of working in our school's self sustaining candle making unit, where in we could utilise our childhood experiences and mentor the rest of the kids. My eyes twinkled and for a moment, I uttered, "Why not? This will be a befitting 'giving back' to our school and all the good that it has done for us."

Manan had other plans. He wanted to be an entrepreneur, start his own non-profit venture along with an accountancy firm. For him, NGO was going to be a voluntary association. But, I saw it always in a different light. Since, being a tiny tot, my life was about letting Manan and Mom grow and be happy. My dreams always stood second. First and most paramount was Manan's life and dreams. His education, his MBA dreams and now his business aspirations.

I instantly convinced Manan to focus on his accountancy firm; meanwhile I would start visiting school unit. My next request to Athavale madam was, "Sorry madam, but what if I also add an art or painting unit to the candle making department? That will also help in generating more revenue for our school's underprivileged children support fund."

Madam was unable to control her tears and gave me a hug. With a teary husk she uttered, "Beta, you have made me the proudest teacher today. When I look at where you came from and what you have become, I can confidently affirm that none of my other students have shaped their character as finely as you have done despite having many more resources and comforts that you never were privileged even to imagine."

I felt like a hero that day. My intent to join the school unit atleast part time was unwavering and in the remaining half, I was going to continue my gallery job.

Manan's business plan was ready and needless to say, he needed funds. He was going to start this venture with one of his best friends from college, who was sufficiently moneyed and was going to invest almost 75% in the business. Manan's role was to look after the entire administration , get clients, employ accountants and delegate work. In short, he was going to be the captain of the ship with support from his friend.

Manan and I started looking for additional investors and found two in our neighbours itself. One evening, we met for tea at our place and discussed the proposition. Our neighbour, Shinde aunty and uncle decided to invest 1.5 lakhs in Manan's firm. We couldn't believe his words. It would have taken us together atleast a year to earn that amount which they were ready to shell out in a moment. I think, we had earned our credibility due to hours and hours of work along with mainstream studies.

Meanwhile, my visits to the school unit started getting regularised. Without a doubt, I can aver that this was the best chapter of my life.

From an empty handed altruist, who just wanted his brother to be a big man one day, I was now part of so many destitute kids' lives teaching them candle making and not just filling candles with colours but their lives too!

The empty handed days were what shaped me wholesomely as a young guy who valued and still holds dear, compassion and charity to all the needy without any judgement or discrimination. I was kind of in a better position, with a degree, a part time job, a social care mission and lot of love and cheer from my family, friends and teachers. But, associating with my school as a volunteer artist made me feel replete and brimming with hope, optimism and motivation. Till then, I had not read theories about the power of giving but felt it piece by piece, bone by bone.

It is now that my concern for the well being of others or what is refinedly called as "Altruism" was growing in leaps and bounds.

What is Success? Being an Altruist or an Artist?

It will be almost ten years since I started volunteering in my school. Life has burgeoned and so has this small school unit. It has become self sustaining, providing recreation, experience and small financial incentives for the kids involved. I am almost 35 years old now and I no longer do this part time job in the gallery. It was my saviour for almost 8 years during my undergraduation and beyond.

A time comes, though, in everybody's life, when they have to break the shackles, literally, take the plunge to achieve the dreams and I had to take mine. I hesitantly met my gallery manager, Mr.Joshi, for evening tea on a Saturday and slowly told him about my future plans to work as an artist full time and how keen I was to start my own painting exhibitions and tours. Joshi sir, for a change, was not angry or moody. He instantly said, "Ok. Manas. I have seen the way you have struggled.

You have been honest always and gave your best here. So, I wish you well for your future artistic journey. Make us all proud."

I touched his feet, filled my heart with all the lovely memories I had as a young budding, gallery executive, came out of the gallery premises, looked at the paintings for the last time as an employee and went off to the school for my voluntary work.

The kids at school, in their brown uniforms, reminded me of Manan and me. We used to wear the same uniform for a week, wash it and use it for days together. Now, times have drastically changed.

Manan has couple of nice formal suits, shirts and trousers. I have a decent collection of clothes. It is so natural to get carried away by this success. When we did not have food and clothes, survival was the only goal. When we have all of that we still crave more but what? Appreciation, success, accolades and more growth. Does this greed end anywhere?

Not really. When I look at Manan today and his incredible growth as an accountant one corner of my mind gets a bit apprehensive.

What if Manan forgets his roots and his battles and starts believing that prosperity is only what matters? I keep subtly telling him to visit the school unit as and when he can and try to shape the lives of hundreds of underprivileged kids that are facing troubles, varying in intensity and type, from what we went through, but nevertheless under immense pressure at that tender age.

Manan has grown into this young, ambitious gentleman, wearing suits, speaking fluently in meetings and contributing effectively towards his business. So many times, gazing at him gives me a feeling of completely mind boggling magic. A ruffled hair, unkempt boy crying for milk to this polished, young budding businessman with extreme passion for his work and exuding an undeniable charm, his journey itself speaks volumes.

I mean, if they take a poll about Manan's top fan, I will ace the list. Right from the way, he dresses to the way he prioritises, he has come of age. For an elder brother who is more like a father, seeing his transformation is the best tonic for me.

Today, I am heading towards my first solo exhibition. The series is named, "Change." I have always believed in creating painting breathing the oxygen of my experiences, sentiments and inner journeys. Change is a series of black and white pencil sketches, about 25 of them. Each speaks its own story right from my birth to Manan's to highlights of a school to the fancies of an artist. My favourite paintings are more than few in this series. I cried for almost 15 minutes looking at the agony on my mother's face in the sketch that shows a red shawl on her and an emaciated baby on her side, my Manan.

There is one painting, which is extremely dear to my soul. Manan is a young kid and I am a grown teenager, both holding hands and just walking on the door, the end of which is a placard called as "Our dreams."

My dreams have literally been resurrected on paper and I feel, these sketches are as live as my joys and sorrows. That is the power of art. It makes you feel cathartic, perceptive and living. All the unsaid experiences in the deepest corner of your heart circulate through your thoughts, to your brain and the tip of your hands.

The exhibition was for 5 days at a well known gallery in Pune. I was fortunate to receive a very good foot fall, almost 5000 people visited my exhibition and majority of them liked my paintings. The dollop on my cake was a first page coverage in the prominent newspaper, "Sakal". The title of the article, "A street boy dared to dream" just churned my intestines so much; I had never felt this contented, excited and proud. The journalist, Paresh, had just written such an immaculate piece, touching upon all the sensitive points that an article about an artist with a challenging life must possess.

I have become a known artist atleast in my city. I have taken a small office space for my art work in the heart of Pune.

I have employed two of the four street children that are students of my school. They are extremely passionate about sketching as well.

Everyday, they assist me in mounting my board, getting my stationery ready and have heaps of questions to ask about why I choose a particular topic, what inspires me, how could I come so far from that hell hole and so on. I don't have a long answer. I say, "Manan's hunger, Mom's vulnerability and my resolve to give them a better existence."

At their young age, they seem to percolate these hard hitting emotions really well.

I was super proud of these tots and their high emotional quotient. Experts claim, Intelligence Quotient, matters. But Emotional Quotient creates the difference. Understanding what the other person needs or what can make his or her day is what I held dear to me and my aspirations all my life. Manan's sorrows became mine; my felicity was out of his achievements primarily.

Now, the essence of young Manan is replicated in all my school unit kids, who so innocently and passionately, make candles, are overjoyed to see the multiple colours on them and try their hand at sketching and colouring.

Art can consume you, positively. They are so engrossed in daily work and are always willing to go that extra mile to create a candle that I love or a sketch that makes me feel nostalgic and proud.

Children and their cherubic existence is what is really giving me all the hope and motivation to draw and create more and more.

This sharing on an emotional and creative level is higher and precious than all the accolades and financial gains clubbed together.

They elicit a response that is full of love and compassion. In the childhood realm, they are the empty handed altruists, who have nothing in cash or kind, but they give and give with full might.

All my life, I had given, not asked. I had cared, not expected. I had rejoiced Manan's success not mine. I am now living the hundred children's dreams and being with them is like the best gift ever that Almighty has bestowed. In retrospection, I feel being born on the street was the purest blessing in disguise.

It taught me the most realistic yet divine lesson. You are empty handed. But, you can still give, share and spread compassion with your empty hands but filled soul. Truly, for the first time, in my life, I felt proud of my intangible achievement, me representing this world changing ethos, to share when you have less, to be there when you are supportless, to be a pillar when your home is dilapidated.

To be this, 'Empty Handed Altruist (SELF--------LESS).'

Author's Side

A dentist researcher by qualification but a mentor-writer by passion and profession! Being an overseas education Consultant and mentor, Dr. Jyuthica Laghate has wholeheartedly dedicated 16 years of her professional life to teaching English and Verbal Reasoning to students regionally, nationally and globally. Along with teaching and counselling students, she has been a successfully published author having two academic books and one self-help fiction book, "Soul Séances." All the three books have received overwhelming response and top rating by reviewers and readers including Amazon. Her unique style of writing and producing stories that have a didactic element and inclusion of the complexities and multi-layering of human

sentiments and experiences is what makes her stories radiate a different light.

As a writer, she feels it as a moral responsibility to personify written work that is authentic to the roots and derived from experiences that can positively transform human existence from adversity to a state of joy and contentment.

In that regard, she is an innate philosopher-writer who holds her pen as a vehicle of good intention.

Contact Details – Dr. Jyuthica. K. Laghate

Founder, Dr. J's Knowledge Café, Pune, India

Email: jyuths@gmail.com

Mobile: +917447789343